Focus Sound & More

F & Simple Concepts

down
on
in
under

Teach the Sound

TYPICAL AGE RANGE

Development: 2-3
Mastery: 2.5-4

HOW TO SAY THE /f/ SOUND

* The inner border of the lower lip is raised to and touches the upper front teeth.
* Have child blow air out of the mouth forming the /f/ sound.
* Make sure there is no voicing added.

TIP

Tell the child to "Bite Your Bottom Lip" and say the /f/ sound.

Read the Story

F

Step 1. **TEACH** a) **Sound**, b) **Word**, c) **Phrase**

Step 2. **MODEL** *Slowly* and *clearly* read the story out loud.

Step 3. **PROMPT** *Pause* and *encourage* child to repeat.

Sound

First, *say* the beginning sound, "fff". *Pause* and *encourage* child to repeat the sound.

Word

Second, *say* the end of the word, "eet". *Pause* and *encourage* child to repeat.
Third, *say* the complete word and *encourage* child to repeat after you, "f-f-eet".
If child doesn't say it on her own, have her repeat after you *(see sample dialogue).*

Phrase

Finally, *say* the simple phrase. Prompt child to repeat by asking, "What does the frog say? One ff...". *Pause* and *encourage* child to finish the phrase ("one foot, two feet").

SAMPLE DIALOGUE

Word Breakdown (fan)
The /f/ sound is said 2 times, then /an/
The /f/ sound is said 1 time, then /an/
Both sounds are said together, "fan."

Have child repeat every sound.

Adult: f-f
Child: f-f
Adult: fff (pause) an
Child: -an
Adult: Almost, Try Again!
Watch my mouth. ffff

F

Speak With Me

ASK

Can you say, "eeffffff"?

If child struggles saying a clear /f/, review <u>TEACH THE SOUND</u>.
If child says a clear /f/,
it's time to <u>SPEAK WITH ME</u>!

INSTRUCTIONS

1- Sit face-to-face with child to show proper modeling of the /f/ sound.
2- Start by pronouncing the beginning sound, pausing,
then pronouncing the ending sound. Have the child repeat after you.
3- Slowly eliminate the pause until the sounds are said together.
4- Don't forget to **praise** a child with **encouraging phrases**
such as: "Good Try," "Great Effort," "Nice Sound!"

Sit Face-to-Face

BEGINNING F

f (pause) ee (*ee* as in *see*)
f (pause) i (*i* as in *fine*)
f (pause) o (*o* as in *no*)
f (pause) um (*um* as in *some*)

ENDING F

aw (pause) f (*aw* as in *ball*)
a (pause) f (*a* as in *dad*)
ee (pause) f (*ee* as in *see*)
oo (pause) f (*oo* as in *too*)

MIDDLE F

aw - f - aw (*aw* as in *ball*)
a - f - a (*a* as in *dad*)
ee - f - ee (*ee* as in *see*)
oo - f - oo (*oo* as in *too*)

PRAISE! BE PATIENT! HAVE FUN!

Fat Freddy's Afraid to Fall

by Angela Holzer, MA
illustrated by Barclay Tucker

Speak With Me Books is a trademark of Good Sound Publishing. www.GoodSoundPublishing.com

Dedicated to Freddy and Joyous (Dad and Mom). Thank you for all your support!

For information please address Good Sound Publishing, Palo Alto CA.94303.

Library of Congress Control Number: 2008909931
ISBN-13, 978-0-9821563-4-6 ----- ISBN-10, 0-9821563-4-0

For Information about **Speak With Me Books** or other products, please visit us at www.SpeakWithMeBooks.com.

This is Fat Freddy,
and he's afraid to fall.

But his favorite food
fell
down
the
wall.

Oh what a fuss
Fat Freddy made.
If only he wasn't
afraid.

1 foot, 2 feet...
nope, too far.

He thinks it's common sense and threw down

a fence.

1 foot, 2 feet...
nope, too far.

But he has a plan and threw down

a fan,
on
a fence.

1 foot, 2 feet...
nope, too far.

He made a wish and threw down

a fish,
on
a fan,
on
a fence.

1 foot, 2 feet...
nope, too far.

He’s all alone and threw down

a phone,
on
a fish,
on
a fan,
on
a fence.

1 foot, 2 feet...
nope, too far.

He doesn't like pork and threw down

a fork,
on
a phone,
on
a fish,
on
a fan,
on
a fence.

1 foot, 2 feet...
nope, too far.

He sat for an hour and threw down

a flower,
on
a fork,
on
a phone,
on
a fish,
on
a fan,
on
a fence.

1 foot, 2 feet...
nope, too far.

He found ten eyes and threw down

five flies,
on
a flower,
on
a fork,
on
a phone,
on
a fish,
on
a fan,
on
a fence.

1 foot,
2 feet...

And then his face. 3 feet, 4 feet,
in just the right place...

on
five flies,
on
a flower,
on
a fork,
on
a phone,
on
a fish,
on
a fan,
on
a fence.

Finally, Fat Freddy found his favorite food…
on the floor,
by a flower,
under the fig tree,
in a hole.

And he ate until he was full.

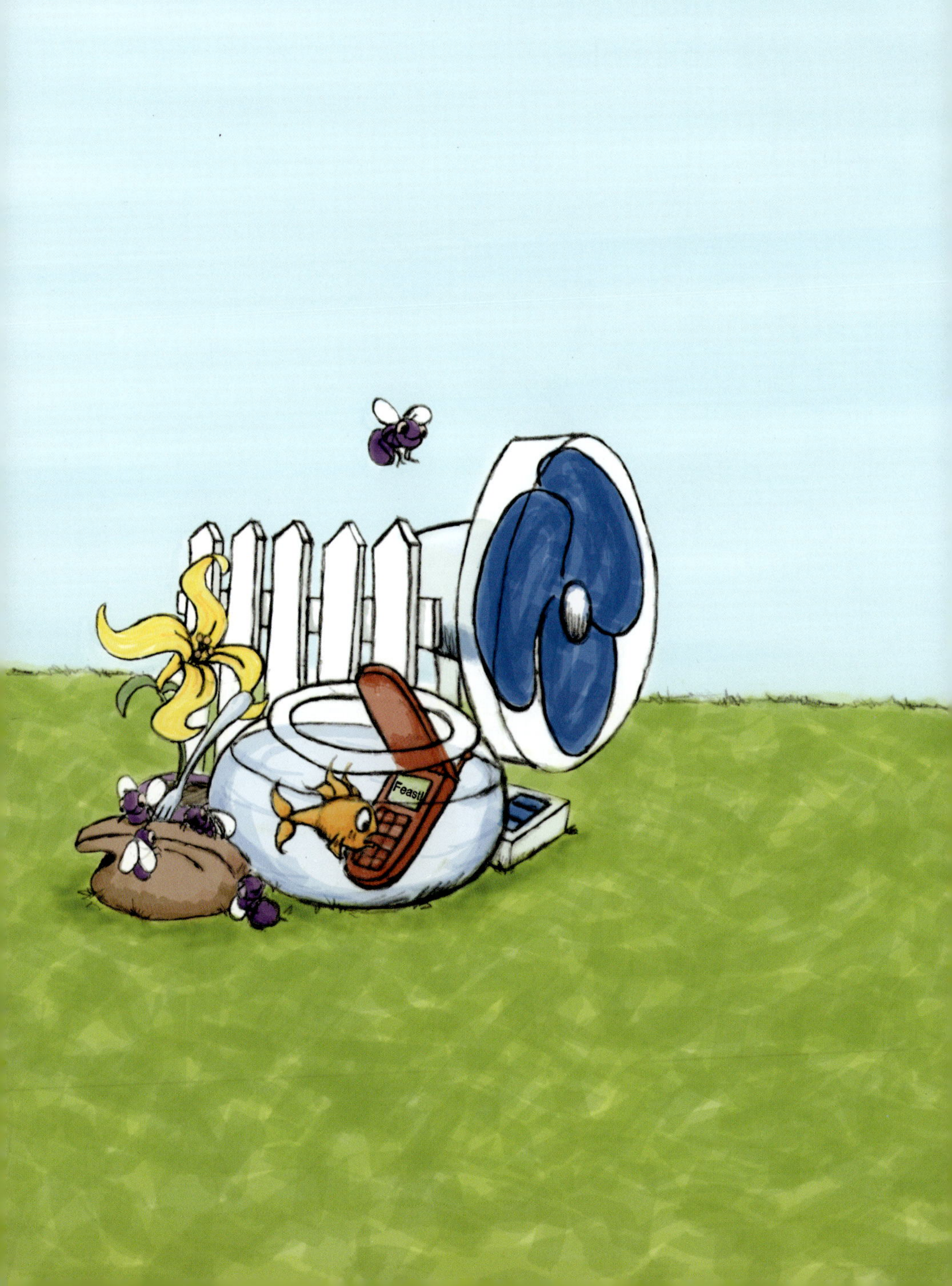

Mmmmmmmmmmm…
fffffff…udge!!!